VICKI LANSKY'S MICROWAVE COOKING FOR KIDS

SCHOLASTIC INC.

New York · Toronto · London · Auckland · Sydney

D1370826

Other titles by Vicki Lansky:

Feed Me I'm Yours
Taming of the Candy Monster
Fat-Proofing Your Children
Kids Cooking
Sing Along as You Ride Along (book and music tape)
Sing Along Birthday Fun (book and music tape)
Koko Bear Read-Together books

To receive a free copy of the mail-order catalog of Vicki Lansky titles, write to:
Practical Parenting, Deephaven, MN 55391, or call 1-800-255-3379.

Special thanks for recipe testing go to:
Alice O'Hara

Metric conversion thanks go to:
Liz McGowan

NOTE: These recipes have been converted to the metric system for the convenience of Canadian readers. Please note, however, that these recipes have not been tested using the metric measurements.

Photography: Harland Graphics
Art direction and design: Lillian Lovitt
Illustrations: Lillian Lovitt
Editor: Erin McCormack

ISBN 0-590-44203

12 11 10 9 8 7 6 5 4 3 2 1   1 2 3 4 5 6/9

Printed in the U.S.A.

23

First Scholastic printing, November 1991

···TABLE OF CONTENTS···

···BREAKFAST···

Microwave Muffins-for-a-Month
(page 8)

Perfect
Poached
Egg
(page 6)

Scrambled Egg for One
(page 7)

Great "Hands-on" Granola
(page 10)

Cinnamon Biscuit Ring
(page 12)

French Toast
(page 14)

···LUNCH···

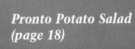

Fast-food Fries
(page 21)

French Onion Soup
(page 22)

Pronto Potato Salad
(page 18)

Octo-Dog
(page 20)

Bacon/Cheese/Tomato Sandwich
(page 16)

···DINNER···

Carrot "Coins"
(page 34)

Meat Loaf "Hole in One"
(page 26)

Make-Ahead Lasagne
(page 28)

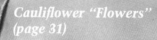

Cauliflower "Flowers"
(page 31)

Chinese Tuna Casserole
(page 30)

Twice-Baked Potatoes
(page 32)

Fried Chicken
(page 24)

·· DESSERT ··

Almond Bark Pieces
(page 42)

Baked Apples
(page 40)

Pineapple Upside-down Cake
(page 36)

Cupcake Cones
(page 38)

Puddle Cake
(page 41)

·SNACKS·

Pizza Tortilla
(page 47)

Bacon Sticks
(page 44)

Nachos
(page 45)

Bananarama
(page 46)

MICROWAVE BASICS

Beware of burning yourself. Food gets hot fast, and heat is also transferred from the food to the cooking dish — which can make the dish hot. Get in the habit of using oven mitts.

Always choose the correct type of cooking dish or pan. Use glass ovenware, Pyrex bowls, microwave-safe ceramic dishes, paper plates, paper cups, glass cups, or anything marked safe for the microwave. Paper towels and waxed paper are appropriate coverings, and so are oven cooking bags if tied with dental floss — not twist-ties.

Set the timer correctly, but stay nearby to rotate or watch what's cooking. Some microwave ovens cook faster than others.

It's important NEVER to have the microwave ON when there is nothing in a dish or container. It can damage the oven.

Combining ingredients in the dish you cook in saves you cleanup time.

See any sparks (or arcing, as it is called) while cooking? Stop cooking and change containers. You picked a non-microwaveable dish. Even twist-ties or metallic trim can cause sparks.

1

WHAT'S DIFFERENT ABOUT A MICROWAVE?

First: Heat, as from an oven or a stove top, doesn't exist here. A microwave cooks by causing food molecules (or tiny, tiny pieces) to vibrate, rub against each other, and create heat by which food cooks or heats up. It's just like when you rub your hands together to warm them up.

Second: Baked foods (breads, cakes, and cookies) also don't brown on the outside because they are not exposed to direct heat. Meats don't brown for the same reason unless they are cooked on a browning dish. That is a dish that can get very hot and brown the food by its touching the surface, which does get hot in a microwave oven.

Third: Foods continue to cook after the oven goes off because it takes time for their molecules' vibrations, caused by the microwaves, to slow down. This is referred to as "standing time." So your food isn't finished cooking until 2 – 5 minutes after the microwave oven stops.

Finally: Microwaves penetrate or hit foods unevenly, depending on the density or thickness of the food, or if it has a high fat content, such as butter. Food edges often cook before the center of the food does, so these tricks help food cook evenly:

- Place foods — such as 6 potatoes — in a circle, leaving an open area in the middle of the circle.

- Create a center empty space with foods, if possible, such as by forming hamburger meat to be cooked into the shape of a doughnut.

- Rotate the dish or the food one-quarter of a turn every 2 minutes while cooking.

> **Assume you will be cooking on high in this cookbook if you have a choice of power levels. Otherwise, just use "on" power.**

Different ovens have different choices of power levels and even different names for different power levels, so just use the highest your oven offers. Just as you would not cook all foods in a regular oven at the highest level, you might wish to experiment with other power levels your oven offers for better results.

HELPFUL TIPS

- Cook packaged convenience foods according to the manufacturer's instructions on the package.

- If your microwave has a turntable, rotating your food will not be necessary, though certain dishes will still need to be stirred.

- Wrapping bread in paper toweling while microwaving prevents it from becoming soggy.

- Before cooking, pierce foods that have a skin or membrane (such as potatoes or hot dogs). A small baked potato will cook in 3 – 4 minutes; a hot dog in a bun and wrapped in a paper towel should take only 30 – 45 seconds.

- When popping corn in a microwave popper or a prepackaged bag, turn off the oven when there is one or two seconds between pops. Don't expect every kernel to pop. Waiting for that to happen will give you burnt popcorn.

- It's not necessary to defrost frozen vegetables before cooking them. With fresh vegetables, it's not necessary to add water to the dish. Just wash off the vegetables (leaving the water on them from the washing), put them in a covered dish, and microwave the appropriate amount of time.

- Poke holes in plastic pouches or wrappings before heating to allow steam to vent, and to prevent plastic from exploding.

- **Never cook in:** Melamine plastic plates, plastic cold-storage containers/plates, or Styrofoam plates UNLESS they are marked "Microwaveable." Don't reuse trays made for one-time convenience products. Also, keep plastic wrap from coming in contact with the food (though it *can* cover a dish if it does not touch the food) unless it, too, is labeled specifically for microwaves.

- **Never cook in:** Metal or aluminum dishes, brown paper bags, or newspaper. Also, don't cover anything with aluminum foil. Glass and paper plates are preferable.

Use a dish only if you know it's microwave safe. If you're not sure, here's how to test it: Place it in the oven next to a one-cup glass measuring cup filled with tap water. Microwave on HIGH for one minute. If the test dish stays cool, it's safe to use. If it's warm, use it only when heating foods for a minute or so. If it's hot, don't use it at all.

BEFORE YOU START

- Be sure to check with an adult about the use of the kitchen.

- Wash your hands before handling food and equipment.

- All equipment should be out and ready before you begin cooking.

- Wear an apron to keep your clothes clean and give you something to wipe your hands on.

- Read through ingredient lists and instructions at least once before you start any recipe.

THINK SAFETY

- Easy-to-reach pot holders or oven mitts are a must, especially when cooking in a microwave oven. The oven will remain "cool," but the food and its cooking dish often become quite hot.

- When removing a lid from a pan, tilt the lid away from you to prevent the hot steam from coming up in your face.

- Place a hot dish from the oven on a wire rack, pot holder, or heatproof surface so it won't damage a counter or table.

- Serrated knives are safer to use than dull knives. Cut away from you and use a cutting board. Never cut anything while holding it in your hand.

- You should never cook with heat (oven, stove top, or microwave) without the knowledge and permission of an adult.

Please read any tip (like this one) at the end of each recipe before you begin. It may give you ideas that you could use in making or serving.

···*Breakfast*···

HERE'S WHAT YOU NEED

(Take out all items before you begin.)

2 Tablespoons (30 mL) water
¼ teaspoon (1 mL) vinegar
1 egg

1 cup or bowl
1 fork
waxed paper
measuring spoons

HERE'S WHAT YOU DO

(First, read steps 1 – 4.)

1. Microwave water and vinegar in a cup or bowl on HIGH for 30 seconds or until boiling.

2. Break egg into cup. Prick yolk with fork. Cover cup with waxed paper.

3. Microwave for 30 to 45 seconds on HIGH.

4. Remove immediately and let stand for 1 minute.

The use of vinegar helps the poached egg keep its shape while cooking.

···*Scrambled Egg for One*···

HERE'S WHAT YOU NEED

(Take out all items before you begin.)

1 teaspoon (5 mL) cottage cheese
1 egg

1 glass cup or bowl
1 spoon or fork
oven mitts
measuring spoons

HERE'S WHAT YOU DO

(First, read steps 1 – 4.)

1. Mix cottage cheese and egg together in a cup or bowl.

2. Microwave on HIGH for 1 minute. (If using a shallow glass dish, reduce cooking time by 10 to 20 seconds.)

3. Stir with spoon or fork and let stand for 1 minute.

4. Eat from the glass or transfer to a plate and serve with toast and orange juice.

Never microwave eggs in their shells. They will explode, and you will have a mess that's difficult to clean up.

Microwave Muffins-for-a-Month

HERE'S WHAT YOU NEED

(Take out all items before you begin.)

4 eggs
1-quart (1-L) container of buttermilk
2 teaspoons (10 mL) vanilla flavoring
3 cups (750 mL) sugar
5 cups (1.25 mL) flour
1 cup (250 mL) cooking oil
5 teaspoons (25 mL) baking soda
1 15- or 20-ounce (475-g)
    box raisin bran cereal

1 very large bowl or
  4-quart (4-L) pot
1 mixing spoon
electric hand beater
large, covered jar or container
custard cups
paper cupcake liners
oven mitts
measuring spoons

HERE'S WHAT YOU DO

(First, read steps 1 – 8.)

1. In a large bowl, beat eggs and vanilla and blend with buttermilk. Add sugar and cooking oil and mix.

2. Combine flour and baking soda and add to above ingredients. Blend well using the electric hand beater.

3. Mix in box of raisin bran cereal. Pour into a large jar or container with a cover.

4. Allow batter to set in the refrigerator for 12 hours before using. (The batter can be stored in refrigerator up to 6 weeks.)

5. Spoon out muffin batter as needed. First line custard cups with cupcake liners, then fill them half full of batter.

6. If more than two cups are being used, place them in a circle in the oven. To make 1 muffin: microwave on HIGH for $1\frac{1}{2}$ minutes. To make 2 muffins: microwave on HIGH for 2 to $2\frac{1}{2}$ minutes. To make 6 muffins: microwave on HIGH for $3\frac{1}{2}$ to $4\frac{1}{2}$ minutes.

7. Using oven mitts, remove custard cups from microwave.

8. To cool, turn over and remove muffins from cups after baking. The muffins will not be brown, but they will taste delicious. Serve with butter or jam.

Make a "muffinloaf" by filling a greased ceramic loaf dish half full. Microwave on HIGH for 5 minutes; give dish a $\frac{1}{4}$ turn and cook for 5 minutes more.

Great "Hands-on" Granola

HERE'S WHAT YOU NEED

(Take out all items before you begin.)

3 cups (750 mL) oatmeal
1 cup (250 mL) untoasted wheat germ
1 cup (250 mL) unsweetened coconut
   (optional)
2 Tablespoons (30 mL) cinnamon
2 Tablespoons (30 mL) brown sugar
¼ cup (50 mL) powdered milk
⅓ cup (75 mL) honey
⅓ cup (75 mL) vegetable oil
1 teaspoon (5 mL) vanilla
Optional: sunflower seeds,
   raisins, dates, or nuts

9" × 13" or 8" × 12"
   (3.5 L) glass dish
1 measuring cup
measuring spoons
1 medium glass bowl
1 large spoon
1 cooling rack or hot plate
1 airtight container
oven mitts

HERE'S WHAT YOU DO

(First, read steps 1 – 8.)

1. Mix all of the dry ingredients together in the large, shallow glass dish.

2. Combine honey, oil, and vanilla in medium glass bowl.

3. Microwave the liquid mixture on HIGH for 30 seconds.

4. Drizzle this warm liquid over the dry ingredients, coating thoroughly, using your hands to mix.

5. Microwave for approximately 9 – 15 minutes on HIGH, stirring every 3 minutes, until granola appears toasty brown.

6. Remove granola from microwave and place on cooling rack or hot plate.

7. Cool completely before removing from dish. Seeds, nuts, raisins, or dates (if desired) should be added after the mixture has cooled.

8. Store in an airtight container.

For breakfast, eat the granola with milk out of a mug instead of a bowl for a change of pace.

···Cinnamon Biscuit Ring···

HERE'S WHAT YOU NEED

(Take out all items before you begin.)

1 8-ounce package (250-g)
  refrigerator crescent rolls

⅓ cup (75 mL) firmly packed
  brown sugar

1 teaspoon (5 mL) cinnamon

3 Tablespoons (45 mL)
  margarine or butter

½ cup (125 mL) chopped nuts
  (pecans or walnuts)

2 Tablespoons (30 mL) water

*1 ceramic, microwave-safe
ring mold (or, you can use
a round 9" [23 cm] pie
plate with a small glass or
glass custard cup turned
upside down in its center)*

1 knife

1 spoon

1 serving plate

1 cooling rack

measuring spoons

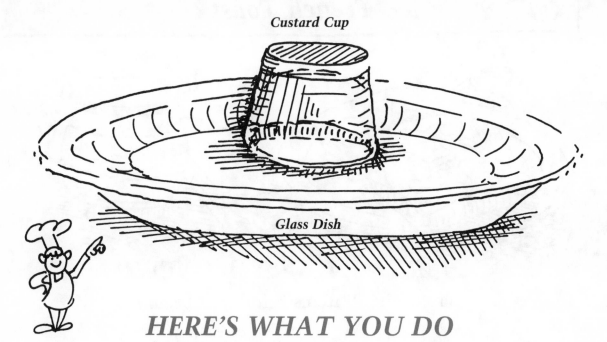

Custard Cup

Glass Dish

HERE'S WHAT YOU DO

(First, read steps 1 – 8.)

1. In ring mold, combine brown sugar, cinnamon, margarine or butter, water, and nuts.

2. Microwave on HIGH for 25 seconds or until margarine or butter is melted. Stir all ingredients until mixed and spread evenly in ring mold.

3. Open the crescent roll package according to directions.

4. Slice the dough cylinder into 8 circles.

5. Place each roll in mixture in ring mold, forming a circle.

6. Microwave uncovered on HIGH for 2 minutes; stop the microwave and rotate the ring mold ½ turn. Then microwave 1 more minute.

7. Remove from oven using pot holders and place on cooling rack.

8. Let ring mold stand for 3 more minutes (set a timer) before inverting onto a serving platter.

To invert, place a serving plate on top of the ring mold, hold in place, and turn upside down. The cinnamon ring will separate neatly from the baking dish onto the serving plate.

HERE'S WHAT YOU NEED

(Take out all items before you begin.)

1 egg
1 Tablespoon (15 mL) milk
2 slices of bread
a drop of vanilla flavoring
Optional: butter, syrup,
  or your favorite jam

1 cereal bowl
1 fork
1 microwave-safe plate
1 spatula
measuring spoons

HERE'S WHAT YOU DO

(First, read steps 1 – 4.)

1. Beat egg, milk, and drop of vanilla flavoring together in a cereal bowl using a fork.

2. Dip each slice of bread in the egg mixture, turning several times until well coated and soaked. Pour balance of liquid on top of each piece.

3. Place bread on plate and microwave 1¼ to 1¾ minutes on HIGH if cooking 1 piece at a time, and 1½ to 2 minutes if cooking 2 pieces together.

4. Flip to serve. Top with butter, syrup, or your favorite jam.

Don't expect this French toast to brown as it would if you were using a stove-top method.

· · · Lunch · · ·

· · · 16 · · ·
•Bacon/Cheese/Tomato Sandwich

· · 18 · · ·
Pronto Potato Salad

· · · 20 · · ·
•Octo-Dog

· · 21 · · ·
Fast-food Fries

· · 22 · · ·
•French Onion Soup

HERE'S WHAT YOU NEED

(Take out all items before you begin.)

2 slices bacon
1 slice bread or a bagel,
  or English muffin, toasted
1 Tablespoon (15 mL)
  mayonnaise or salad dressing
1 slice tomato
1 slice Swiss, cheddar,
  or American cheese

1 shallow glass baking dish
1 knife
2 paper towels
1 plate
measuring spoons

HERE'S WHAT YOU DO

(First, read steps 1 – 6.)

1. Arrange bacon between layers of paper towels in shallow glass baking dish.

2. Microwave on HIGH for 1½ to 2 minutes or until bacon is crisp; set aside.

3. Toast bread, bagel, or muffin and place it on plate.

4. Spread mayonnaise or salad dressing with a knife on the bread. Top with tomato, bacon, and cheese.

5. Microwave, uncovered, 30 seconds or until cheese is melted.

6. Remove from oven and it's ready to eat.

Another helpful hint: You can freshen up soggy potato chips by microwaving on HIGH for 45 seconds (per 2 cups of chips), and letting stand for 1 minute. This also works for pretzels, crackers, or popcorn

HERE'S WHAT YOU NEED

(Take out all items before you begin.)

4 cups (500 g) frozen
  hash brown potatoes
  from a bag (approximately
  ½ of a 32-ounce bag)
⅓ cup (75 mL) water
1 carrot, shredded or grated
½ cup (125 mL) chopped celery
½ cup (125 mL) mayonnaise
1 Tablespoon (15 mL)
  white vinegar
1 Tablespoon (15 mL) sugar

2-quart (1-L) casserole with cover
carrot peeler
1 large spoon
oven mitts
cooling rack or hot plate
measuring spoons

HERE'S WHAT YOU DO

(First, read steps 1 – 8.)

1. Combine 4 cups frozen hash brown potatoes and ⅓ cup water in casserole and cover.

2. Microwave on HIGH for 6 minutes. Stir, then microwave for another 3 to 6 minutes or until potatoes are tender.

3. Remove covered dish from the oven using mitts and place on cooling rack or hot plate.

4. Remove cover and let the potatoes cool.

5. While the potatoes are cooling, peel, then grate the carrot. Chop up ½ cup of celery and add it with the carrot to top of potatoes.

6. Combine mayonnaise, vinegar, and sugar together, mixing thoroughly.

7. Add above mixture to potatoes, carrots, and celery; mix thoroughly.

8. Chill before serving.

Use an ice-cream scoop to make attractively shaped servings on a plate.

· · · Octo-Dog · · ·

HERE'S WHAT YOU NEED

(Take out all items before you begin.)

1 hot dog
Optional: ketchup, mustard,
   or pickle relish

1 medium-size drinking glass
   (made of glass)
1 paper plate
1 wooden popsicle stick
1 serving plate
oven mitts
1 knife

HERE'S WHAT YOU DO

(First, read steps 1 – 4.)

1. Slice hot dog halfway down the middle lengthwise; turn and slice again so you have four "legs." (See illustration.)

2. Insert wooden popsicle stick into the middle of the unsliced portion of the hot dog.

3. Place down inside a drinking glass with "legs" hanging over the top of the glass sides. Have the glass sit on small paper plate to catch fat drippings.

4. Microwave on HIGH for 1 minute or less. Use oven mitts to remove from oven. Lift hot dog from glass using the wooden stick.

Hot dogs cook quickly because of their high fat content.

HERE'S WHAT YOU NEED

(Take out all items before you begin.)

Bag of frozen shoe-string fries
Optional: ketchup

1 paper coffee filter
(triangle shape or round),
folded in half

HERE'S WHAT YOU DO

(First, read steps 1 – 4.)

1. Place frozen fries side by side in a single layer inside the coffee filter.

2. Microwave on HIGH for 1 minute, then flip paper filter containing potatoes over, and microwave 1 more minute.

3. Remove from the oven and turn down the edges of the paper filter to make a fast-food serving container.

4. Add ketchup if desired.

The foods we eat contain more sodium than is necessary. Here is an easy place to avoid using extra salt.

··· *French Onion Soup* ···

HERE'S WHAT YOU NEED

(Take out all items before you begin.)

1 can beef broth or French onion soup
2 Tablespoons (30 mL) chopped onion
2 Tablespoons (30 mL) butter
2 1-inch slices of French bread, toasted
2 slices Swiss cheese

can opener
2 microwave-safe soup bowls
1 knife
1 spoon
measuring spoons

HERE'S WHAT YOU DO

(First, read steps 1 – 4.)

1. Place 1 Tablespoon of chopped onion and 1 Tablespoon of butter in each bowl. Microwave on HIGH for 1 minute or until onion is translucent or looks clear. Stir butter and onion together and set bowls aside.

2. Dilute soup according to directions on the can and pour over the onions, dividing it evenly between the 2 bowls. Microwave the soup on HIGH for 1 minute.

3. Put one slice of toasted French bread on the top of each bowl of soup, and then top each with a slice of cheese.

4. Microwave on HIGH for 30 seconds or until the cheese has melted.

When microwaving liquids, never fill the bowl or cup to the top because the liquid will bubble over.

· · ·Dinner· · ·

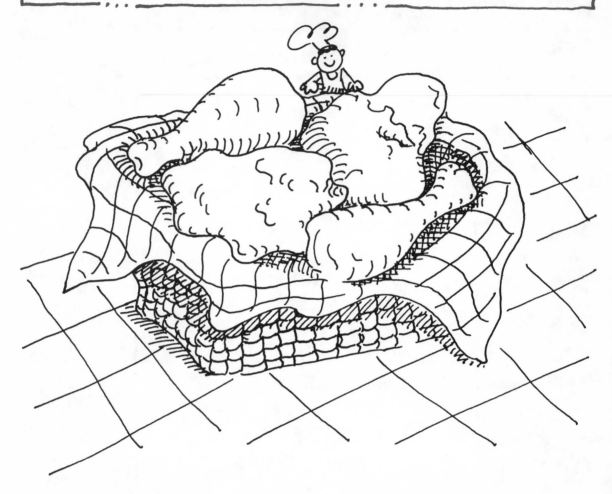

HERE'S WHAT YOU NEED

(Take out all items before you begin.)

2 cups (500 mL) Rice Krispies cereal
1 envelope Good Seasons
 Italian Salad Dressing mix
2 Tablespoons (30 mL)
 margarine or butter
1 2½- to 3-pound (1.25 kg.)
 broiler-fryer chicken, cut up
Optional: ¼ cup (50 mL)
 toasted wheat germ

1 12" × 7½" × 2" (3 L)
 baking dish with
 microwave-safe rack, or a
 glass-covered casserole dish
paper or cloth towel
1 large plastic bag
1 large glass measuring cup
1 piece of waxed paper
measuring spoons

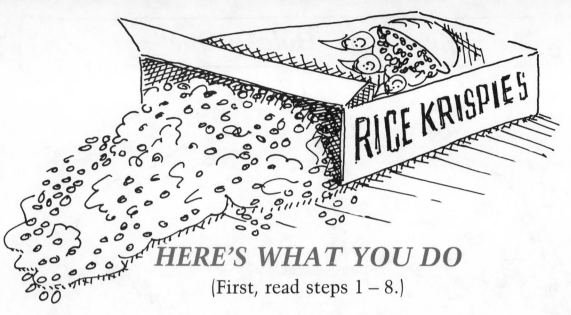

HERE'S WHAT YOU DO

(First, read steps 1 – 8.)

1. Tear the skin off of the chicken pieces. Rinse the chicken well under running water. Pat the pieces dry with a paper or cloth towel.

2. Place the cereal in a plastic bag and gently pound the bag with the bottom of the glass measuring cup to crush the cereal.

3. Add the Good Seasons Italian Salad Dressing mix and wheat germ to the crushed cereal. Shake bag to mix.

4. In the baking dish, microwave the margarine or butter, uncovered, on HIGH 15 to 45 seconds or until melted. Place the chicken pieces in the dish to coat them on all sides with the melted butter.

5. Put chicken, 1 or 2 pieces at a time, into the bag with crushed cereal mixture. Shake to coat.

6. Place the coated chicken pieces back into the baking dish. Arrange chicken with the meatiest portions toward the outside of dish.

7. Sprinkle some of the remaining crushed cereal mixture on top of the coated chicken. Cover dish with waxed paper.

8. Microwave on HIGH for 10 minutes and then give dish ½ turn and cook another 10 minutes. Remove with oven mitts and let stand for 3 – 5 minutes before serving.

Use a tall glass or bottle as a rolling pin to crush the cereal in the plastic bag.

HERE'S WHAT YOU NEED

(Take out all items before you begin.)

2 pounds (1 kg) ground beef
1 egg
½ cup (125 mL) bread crumbs,
  plain or seasoned
½ cup (125 mL) water
1 envelope dry onion-soup
  mix from 2.4-ounce (70-g) box
Bottle of chili sauce or
  barbeque sauce

*1 microwave-safe ceramic ring
  mold or 1 round glass pie dish*
1 large spoon or hand masher
1 large mixing bowl
1 cup or larger measuring cup
1 knife
serving plate
oven mitts

HERE'S WHAT YOU DO

(First, read steps 1 – 8.)

1. Unwrap the ground beef package and place in a large mixing bowl.

2. Crack the egg and drop it into the bowl with the ground beef. Add ½ cup bread crumbs to the ground beef.

3. Fill the measuring cup with ½ cup of water and add contents of 1 envelope of dry onion-soup mix. Stir briefly and then add to ground beef.

4. Now mix all ingredients well with the ground beef. You may prefer to use your hands (clean, of course) to "squeeze" the mixture, instead of the spoon or masher.

5. Shape the meat mixture into a ring around the edge of the pie plate leaving a "hole" in the middle.

6. Pour some chili sauce or barbeque sauce over the top of this meat "ring." Use a knife to spread it evenly over the meat.

7. Microwave on HIGH for 10 minutes. Remove from oven, using oven mitts, and carefully remove some of the excess liquid fat by pouring or spooning it into a metal can. Return meat to microwave for another 5 minutes on HIGH.

8. Remove from oven with oven mitts and again remove excess liquid fat. If the meat looks too pink when you slice it, return it to the microwave for another 2 – 3 minutes. Then slide meat loaf ring onto a serving dish.

> *Put rice, mashed potatoes, or vegetables in the center hole when serving.*

HERE'S WHAT YOU NEED

(Take out all items before you begin.)

30- to 32-ounce (796-mL) jar
  of spaghetti sauce
8-ounce (250-g) package
  of uncooked lasagne noodles
1½ cups (375 mL) cottage cheese
3 cups (750 mL) shredded mozzarella
  cheese (12-ounce package)
water

8" × 12", or 9" × 13"
  (3.5 L) glass baking dish
1 medium bowl
big spoon
1 knife
oven mitts
plastic wrap

HERE'S WHAT YOU DO

(First, read steps 1 – 8.)

1. Soak uncooked lasagne noodles in the baking dish with hot tap water for about 5 minutes, or while you're getting the other ingredients together. Remove noodles from water and place on the kitchen counter or in another dish.

2. Use about 1/3 of the spaghetti sauce to cover the bottom of the baking dish.

3. Spread 1/2 of the wet, uncooked noodles in a layer lengthwise on the sauce.

4. Cover the sauce with 1/2 of the cottage cheese.

5. Add 1/2 of the shredded mozzarella cheese over the cottage cheese.

6. Repeat steps 2, 3, and 4, using a spoon or a knife to spread the last 1/3 of the spaghetti sauce over the cheese.

7. Cover with plastic wrap and place in refrigerator **overnight**.

8. Vent one corner of the plastic wrap by folding it up and microwave on HIGH for 20 minutes. Let it stand for 15 minutes before cutting and serving.

Crumbled, cooked ground beef can be added to the spaghetti sauce for a heartier meal.

··· Chinese Tuna Casserole ···

HERE'S WHAT YOU NEED

(Take out all items before you begin.)

2 6½-ounce cans (184 g) tuna,
  drained
1 10¾-ounce can (284 mL) cream
  of mushroom or celery soup
¼ cup (50 mL) milk
1⅓ cups (100 g) chow mein noodles
  (save ⅓ cup for topping)
1 cup (250 mL) chopped celery
Optional: ½ cup (125 mL)
  sliced water chestnuts

can opener
1 1½-quart casserole dish
1 spoon
oven mitts
cooling rack or hot plate

HERE'S WHAT YOU DO

(First, read steps 1 – 4.)

1. Mix drained tuna, undiluted soup, milk, 1 cup chow mein noodles, celery, and water chestnuts in casserole dish.

2. Cover with plastic wrap, leaving one corner open, and microwave 5 minutes on HIGH.

3. Remove from oven with mitts and let stand on a cooling rack.

4. Sprinkle top evenly with remaining chow mein noodles.

Serve with fortune cookies to complete the theme of the meal.

···Cauliflower "Flowers"···

HERE'S WHAT YOU NEED

(Take out all items before you begin.)

1 lemon
1 head of cauliflower
3 – 4 Tablespoons (45 – 60 mL)
   of butter or margarine
½ cup (125 mL) bread crumbs

1 glass baking dish — 10" (25 cm)
   pie plate or an 8" × 10" (2 L) dish
2 cereal bowls
plastic wrap
measuring spoons

HERE'S WHAT YOU DO

(First, read steps 1 – 4.)

1. Wash cauliflower and cut away the leaves and core. Separate the cauliflower clumps into separate "flowers."

2. Put bread crumbs in one bowl and butter in the other. Melt butter in the microwave on HIGH for 30 seconds.

3. Dip each "flower" first in butter and then in bread crumbs. Place in baking dish. Cover with plastic wrap, leaving one corner vented.

4. Microwave on HIGH for 3½ minutes.

Cut up a lemon into wedges and serve with the cauliflower.

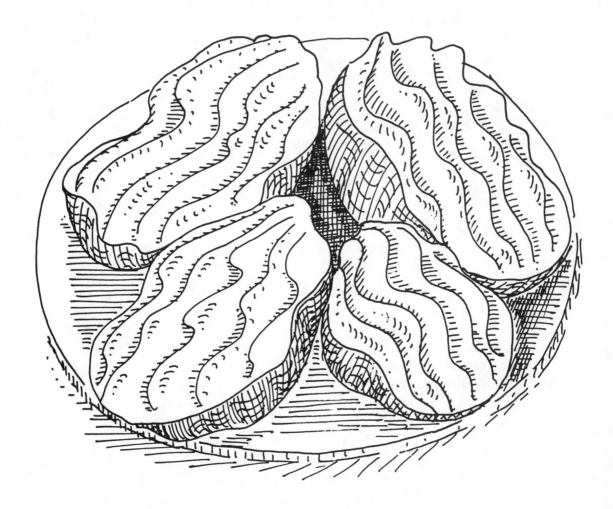

HERE'S WHAT YOU NEED

(Take out all items before you begin.)

1 large baking potato
1 Tablespoon (15 mL) butter or margarine,
 plus two dabs
1 Tablespoon (15 mL) milk
1 Tablespoon (15 mL) shredded
 cheddar cheese

1 paper towel
1 fork
1 knife
1 medium bowl
1 spoon or grapefruit spoon
measuring spoons

HERE'S WHAT YOU DO
(First, read steps 1 – 8.)

1. Scrub potato and then pierce with fork twice, once on each end.

2. Wrap the potato in a paper towel and microwave on HIGH for 3 – 5 minutes or until potato no longer feels hard. ("Test" quickly with fingers as potato will be hot.)

3. Let the potato stand for another 10 minutes to complete cooking and cool down.

4. Slice the potato into two parts by cutting it lengthwise with a sharp knife.

5. Use a spoon to scoop out the inside of the potato halves into a bowl. Set the skins aside.

6. Mix the potato insides with 1 Tablespoon each of butter, milk, and cheese. Mash with fork until smooth.

7. Refill the potato skins with the mixture. Dab each top with butter.

8. Microwave potato halves on a plate on HIGH for 1 minute.

Sprinkle artificial bacon bits, paprika, or chives on top before the last return to the oven. Sour cream is also a favorite extra topping when served.

···Carrot "Coins"···

HERE'S WHAT YOU NEED

(Take out all items before you begin.)

3 or 4 large carrots
2 Tablespoons (30 mL)
   butter or margarine
Optional: parsley

1 covered casserole dish
1 knife
1 cutting board
1 spoon
oven mitts

HERE'S WHAT YOU DO

(First, read steps 1 – 4.)

1. Scrub carrots and cut off their ends. On a cutting board, slice carrots approximately every ¼ inch to make "coins."

2. Transfer carrots to casserole dish and add butter.

3. Cover the casserole and microwave on HIGH for 5 to 6 minutes or until tender.

4. Stir the carrots and butter, and sprinkle with parsley.

Most vegetables cook in less than five minutes. Corn on the cob can even be microwaved right in the husk, or you can try wrapping each ear in a paper towel after you have removed the outer husk and silk.

· · · *Dessert* · · ·

· · · Pineapple Upside-down Cake · · ·

HERE'S WHAT YOU NEED
(Take out all items before you begin.)

1 18½-ounce (500-g) package
   of yellow or white cake mix
1 can pineapple rings (4 or 5 slices)
½ cup (125 mL) brown sugar
2 Tablespoons (30 mL)
   margarine or butter
maraschino cherries

8" square or 8½" (2 L)
   round glass pan
1 bowl
1 mixing spoon
1 fork
measuring spoons

HERE'S WHAT YOU DO

(First, read steps 1 – 8.)

1. Mix the cake mix according to directions, substituting juice from the can of pineapple rings for part of the liquid required.

2. Put margarine and brown sugar in pan and melt in microwave for 25 seconds.

3. Remove pan from oven; mix well. Spread evenly over bottom of pan.

4. Lift pineapple rings from can one by one to drain; arrange them to cover bottom of pan in single layer.

5. Place a red cherry in the center hole of each pineapple ring and one in the center of the dish.

6. Spoon ½ of cake batter over pineapple slices, filling dish only ½ way up sides.

7. Microwave on HIGH for 8 minutes, turning the dish ¼ turn every 2 minutes.

8. Remove using oven mitts. Let cake stand 5 minutes and then turn cake upside down on a serving plate.

Use balance of batter to make individual cupcake cones on the next page.

HERE'S WHAT YOU NEED

(Take out all items before you begin.)

1 box white or yellow cake mix:
   18-ounce (500-g) box will make
   24 cones
   9-ounce (250-g) box will make
   12 cones
1 box of flat-bottomed ice-cream cones
Homemade frosting (for 12 cones):
   2 cups (500 mL) confectioners' sugar
   1/3 cup (75 mL) Crisco or softened
   margarine
   1 teaspoon (5 mL) vanilla flavoring
   2 Tablespoons (30 mL) milk

1 large mixing bowl
1 medium mixing bowl
1 mixer or a large spoon
measuring spoons
1 knife

HERE'S WHAT YOU DO

(First, read steps 1 – 8.)

1. Prepare cake mix as directed on package.

2. Open package of cones and stand them separately on a flat surface.

3. Place 2 Tablespoons of cake batter in each cone.

4. Microwave 2 cones at a time on HIGH power for 45 seconds.

5. Remove each pair of cupcake cones from the oven and let cool on flat surface.

6. In a medium bowl, combine Crisco or margarine, confectioners' sugar, vanilla, and milk. Mix on low speed for 30 seconds and then on high until ingredients are creamy. (If the frosting appears hard or dry, add an extra Tablespoon of milk and mix again.)

7. To make different-colored cones, separate the white frosting in 2 or 3 small bowls, add one or two drops of food coloring to each bowl, and mix.

8. Use a knife to spread the frosting on top of your cooled cupcake cones.

Frost cones with different colors to give the appearance of different "flavors" of ice cream.

· Baked Apple ·

HERE'S WHAT YOU NEED
(Take out all items before you begin.)

1 large apple
1 Tablespoon (15 mL)
   of frozen apple-juice concentrate
cinnamon stick

1 sharp knife
1 apple corer
1 microwave-safe cereal
   bowl or custard cup
oven mitts
measuring spoons

HERE'S WHAT YOU DO
(First, read steps 1 – 4.)

1. Level apple by slicing off a very small section horizontally across the bottom. Then slice horizontally across the top to make a cut-off cap. Set it aside and core the main part of the apple.

2. Place the apple in the dish and spoon the apple juice concentrate into the apple's center.

3. Place the "cap" on the apple and secure it down the middle with a cinnamon stick. Microwave on HIGH for 2½ to 3 minutes (4 apples, placed in a circle, will take 5 minutes).

4. Remove using an oven mitt, and let stand for at least 1 more minute before serving.

A grapefruit spoon works well for eating a baked apple—hot or chilled.

···*Puddle Cake*···

HERE'S WHAT YOU NEED

(Take out all items before you begin.)

1½ cups (375 mL) flour (white or
    half white, half whole wheat)
1 cup (250 mL) sugar
1 teaspoon (5 mL) baking soda
3 Tablespoons (45 mL)
    cocoa or carob powder
1 teaspoon (5 mL) vanilla flavoring
1 teaspoon (5 mL) vinegar
6 Tablespoons (90 mL) cooking oil
1 cup (250 mL) water
confectioners' sugar

1 8" × 10" (2 L) glass cake pan
1 fork
oven mitts
cooling rack
measuring spoons

HERE'S WHAT YOU DO

(First, read steps 1 – 4.)

1. Combine flour, sugar, soda, and cocoa into an ungreased cake pan. With a
   fork, mix ingredients together thoroughly.

2. Using fork, make three holes in the dry mixture. Pour vanilla in the first
   hole, vinegar in the second, and oil in the third. Pour water over all and stir
   with a fork to moisten dry ingredients.

3. Microwave on HIGH for 6 minutes or until middle is cooked, turning cake
   ¼ turn every 2 minutes.

4. Remove from oven using oven mitts and place on cooling rack. Wait until
   the cake has cooled and sprinkle with confectioners' sugar.

*For a quick frosting, pour 1 cup of chocolate chips on top of the cake while
it is still warm. After chips have melted, use a knife to spread them
around evenly.*

··· Almond Bark Pieces ···

HERE'S WHAT YOU NEED

(Take out all items before you begin.)

1 16-ounce (500-g.) package
  of chocolate bark
1 6-ounce (170-g) bag of slivered,
  sliced, or whole almonds

1 mixing spoon or knife
1 knife
waxed paper
cookie sheet
glass dish

HERE'S WHAT YOU DO

(First, read steps 1 – 4.)

1. Place all squares of chocolate bark in a glass dish. (Some bark may even come in a microwaveable oven tray.)

2. Microwave on HIGH for 1 minute, stirring well. Continue microwaving at 15-second intervals, stirring after each interval until the candy is smooth. (Chocolate bark retains its shape while melting, so only by stirring it will you know when all the pieces have melted completely.)

3. Add almonds to the mixture and stir carefully until all the nuts are covered.

4. Cover cookie sheet with waxed paper and spread mixture over it to desired thickness. Let it cool until firm, then cut or break into pieces.

Store pieces, wrapped, in the freezer for a particularly nice crunchy treat.

··· Snacks ···

··· *44* ···
Bacon Sticks

··· *45* ···
Nachos

··· *46* ···
Bananarama

··· *47* ···
Pizza Tortilla

···*Bacon Sticks*···

HERE'S WHAT YOU NEED

(Take out all items before you begin.)

5 strips of bacon
5 bread sticks

3 paper towels
1 long, shallow glass dish
knife or scissors
serving dish

HERE'S WHAT YOU DO

(First, read steps 1 – 4.)

1. Place 2 paper towels in the bottom of a glass dish.

2. Slice one piece of bacon in half lengthwise and then wrap the less fatty piece around one bread stick, making it twist from top to bottom like a barbershop pole. Lay the bacon stick in the glass dish.

3. Repeat step 2 for remaining bread sticks.

4. Place a second paper towel on top of bacon sticks and microwave on HIGH for 2 minutes, or until bacon is crisp.

Sprinkle the bacon sticks with parmesan cheese for a nice flavor.

··· *Nachos* ···

HERE'S WHAT YOU NEED
(Take out all items before you begin.)

½ package — 7 ounces or
about 5 cups (200 g)
— tortilla chips
1 cup (250 mL) grated
cheddar cheese
1 cup (250 mL) salsa

1 8″ × 10″ (2 L) glass baking dish
1 serving dish
1 custard cup or cereal bowl

HERE'S WHAT YOU DO
(First, read steps 1 – 2.)

1. Spread tortilla chips evenly into baking dish and sprinkle with cheese.
   Microwave on HIGH for 30 to 45 seconds or until cheese is soft and melty.

2. Put salsa in custard cup as a dip for the nachos and place in the center of the
   serving dish. Arrange nachos on the plate around the salsa and enjoy!

*For variety, microwave a cup of refried beans on HIGH for 1 minute and
serve with your nachos.*

HERE'S WHAT YOU NEED

(Take out all items before you begin.)

1 banana   *1 paper plate*
6 chocolate chips   *knife*
6 mini-marshmallows   *2 toothpicks*
                  spoon

HERE'S WHAT YOU DO

(First, read steps 1 – 4.)

1. Take an *unpeeled* banana and cut *the peel only* lengthwise along the inside curve (see illustration).

2. In the exposed section, cut a V-shaped wedge from the banana (and eat it!).

3. Put the chocolate chips and marshmallow pieces into the wedge and "re-cover" it with the banana peel strip.

4. Place the banana on a plate and run 2 toothpicks through banana about 3 inches apart to keep it from tipping over. Microwave on HIGH for a minute or less. Eat with a spoon.

Don't be put off by the peel turning brown. The banana is delicious inside!

··· *Pizza Tortilla* ···

HERE'S WHAT YOU NEED

(Take out all items before you begin.)

1 round flour tortilla
3 Tablespoons (45 mL)
   prepared pizza sauce
3 Tablespoons (45 mL)
   shredded mozzarella cheese
Optional: dried oregano,
   garlic powder

1 plate or paper plate
measuring spoons
1 knife
1 pizza cutter

HERE'S WHAT YOU DO

(First, read steps 1 – 4.)

1. Remove one tortilla from package and place in center of a paper plate. Close package well (so others don't dry out) and return package to refrigerator.

2. Spread 3 Tablespoons of pizza sauce with a knife evenly around on the tortilla. Then sprinkle with 3 Tablespoons of the cheese.

3. Microwave uncovered on HIGH for 30 to 45 seconds until sauce begins to bubble and cheese looks shiny or has just started to melt.

4. Sprinkle lightly with dried oregano and/or garlic powder, if you like. Use a rolling pizza cutter to cut into pie-shaped pieces.

For variety, substitute an English muffin, which you toast before adding sauce and cheese toppings.

· · · INDEX · · ·